Sometimes It Happens

Someone Special Dies

by
Annette Blake

ISBN: 9798652243289

 For permission requests, write to the publisher.
Published by: YesBear Publishing
info@YesBearPublishing.com

Dedication

I dedicate this book
to the most
precious person in
my life! I love you
Grammie and know
you are a shining
star !
I know every time a
beautiful butterfly
flies by you are here!
Sometimes it
happens ♡

I also want to include the Lopez family
who inspired me to write for their son
Brian. Stars shine up above ☆

You plant a flower
and it never grows!

You buy a fish and
sometimes you
find it afloat.

But sometimes someone special could become sick.

Sometimes they could get better
and be well very quick.

But sometimes
it happens,

And there is no real
answer why?

Sometimes someone
close to you may die.

It could be a grandparent, it could be a friend,

Sometimes it happens, their life has reached an end.

When this sometime happens,
it's okay to be mad!

When this sometime happens,
you will feel sad!

When this sometime happens,
remember to share,

Talk about how you feel and let everybody know you care.

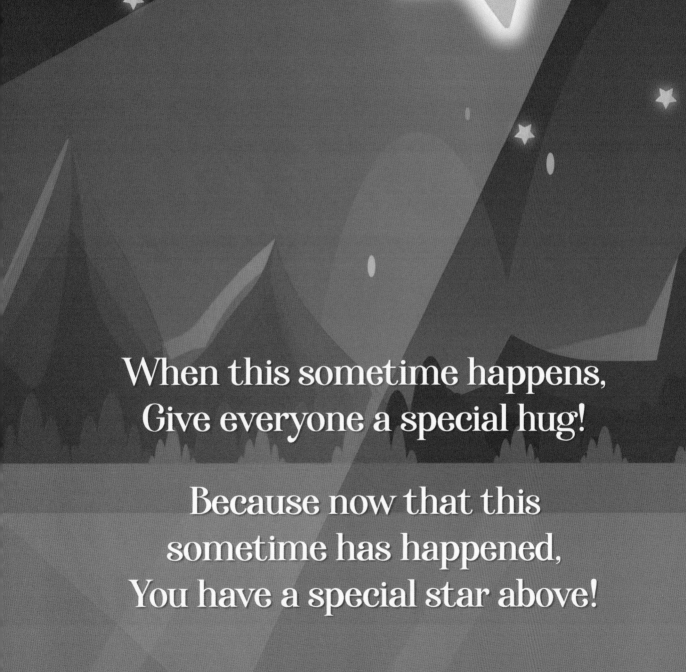

When this sometime happens,
Give everyone a special hug!

Because now that this
sometime has happened,
You have a special star above!

The best thing to do if it happens
is to always remember the smiling face.

Remember the fun times together
and know they are in a safe place.

Because sometimes it happens and every night you go to sleep,

Look to the stars
and know it's okay!

Sometimes It Happens

About the Author

Annette Blake's first book was created when she was an ABA therapist. She was asked by a parent to write a book about someone dying, because her son had just lost one of his friends at age 6. That is how *Sometimes It Happens* began.

She has a Bachelor of Arts degree in Psychology from California State University in Long Beach and an Education in Early Childhood certification from Orange Coast College. Annette has been working with young children for over 30 years. Her many experiences have led her to the goal of her books: *to create simple ways for kids to cope with difficult life situations.*

She lives in Huntington Beach, California where she enjoys spending time with her boyfriend Mike, family and friends. She enjoys boating, gardening and going to the beach. Her favorite hobby is teaching her students.

Sometimes It Happens

Please paste a special
picture of your Sometime!

More from the Author!

Be sure to check out Annette's other
Sometimes It Happens books,
with even more coming soon!

Printed in Great Britain
by Amazon